UNBROKEN SHACKLES

THE SILENT PRISON OF THE MIND

CAPT JAGJIT KHULLAR

Made with ♥ on the Notion Press Platform
www.notionpress.com

Contents

Foreword

Unbroken Shackles: The Silent Prison of the Mind is a profound exploration of the invisible chains that bind us—chains forged by our own thoughts, fears, habits, and societal conditioning. In this transformative narrative, the authors take us on a journey of self-discovery, highlighting the silent battles we all face within our minds and offering actionable wisdom to break free.

Through the engaging dialogue between Amby and Abhishek, the book addresses universal struggles: the weight of expectations, the traps of toxic relationships, financial instability, and the pursuit of meaning in an ever-changing world. Their candid conversations reveal that true freedom is not merely external but a deeply internal conquest—one that begins with awareness, discipline, and a commitment to personal growth.

What makes this book remarkable is its blend of timeless life lessons, practical tools like affirmations and routines, and heartfelt reflections that resonate across cultures and generations. It doesn't just tell us to change—it shows us how, step by step, with sincerity and conviction we can change.

Whether you are at the peak of success or grappling with setbacks, *Unbroken Shackles* offers a roadmap to liberation. It invites you to introspect, reassess, and reclaim your power, encouraging you to embrace life with renewed purpose and passion.

May this book serve as a companion on your journey to breaking free from the silent prison of the mind and unlocking the limitless potential within you.

I have the privilege of knowing Capt. Jagjit Khullar personally. He plays a pivotal role in managing the training needs at Ind-Aust Maritime Pvt. Ltd., Navi Mumbai, and has been deeply involved in training engineering professionals in the Merchant Navy. Capt. Khullar is a well-read individual with an unwavering passion for teaching and writing. His multifaceted personality shines through as a motivational speaker, healer, and an educator also.

I extend my heartfelt congratulations to Capt. Jagjit Khullar for this remarkable accomplishment in his debut literary venture. Entering the realm of Authorpreneurship with such a magnificent work is no small feat, and I sincerely hope this is just the beginning of a long and illustrious journey. May he continue to achieve even greater laurels in the future.

Ms Meena Singh

General Manager,
Ind-Aust Maritime Pvt. Ltd.
Navi Mumbai -400 705

Acknowledgements

This book is dedicated to my family, with special gratitude to my daughter, Gauri, for her invaluable contributions in editing and proofreading. I extend my heartfelt thanks to my near and dear ones, my colleagues, the senior management at Ind-Aust Maritime, and the countless students I have had the privilege to mentor.

I am equally grateful to the visible and invisible supporters who played a crucial role in bringing this dream project to life. Your encouragement, guidance, and efforts have been instrumental in making this book a reality.

To all of you, I offer my sincere thanks and deep appreciation—for without your support, this work would not have been possible.

Lesson ONE

Unbroken Shackles: The Silent Prison of the Mind

Life, in its essence, is not about escaping suffering. It is about growing strong enough to face it head-on. Ironically, the greatest obstacles we face often arise from within ourselves. These are the mental blocks—the self-imposed shackles—that bind us to a cycle of misery and pain. We carry them unknowingly, thinking that life will get easier on its own, but in reality, we must grow stronger to shape life according to our desires.

As we journey through life, these invisible shackles remain. We weave them around ourselves, trapping our potential, without ever fully realizing the true cause of our suffering. The question is: How can we ever hope for a better life if we don't break free from these chains?

The mystery of these shackles begins to unravel through a conversation between Mr. Abhishek and Mrs. Amby, a married couple enjoying a peaceful stroll along a quiet beach in Goa one summer evening. The cool sea breeze ruffled their hair, and the rhythmic sound of the waves crashing against the shore created a serene atmosphere. In this moment of peace, their minds were free of worry, their thoughts unburdened.

Yet, suddenly, a question struck Mrs. Amby's mind, pulling her out of the calm. She turned to her husband, her curiosity piqued.

"Abhishek," she began thoughtfully, "why is it that some people achieve great success while others don't? I mean, look around. People from different backgrounds, cultures, and countries—they all seem to be here for the same thing, to enjoy the moment. Yet, some are here to serve others, and some are here to be served. Why is that? Is it luck?"

Abhishek looked at her, his expression thoughtful. He shook his head slowly. "No, it is not luck or destiny, Amby," he replied. "It's how we've shaped our lives, consciously or unconsciously. Success, or the lack of it, depends on our own choices."

"Are you ready to hear my thoughts on this?" Abhishek asked, his tone shifting to one of contemplation.

"Yes, of course!" Mrs. Amby responded eagerly. "Please, go on. I'm so curious to hear your perspective."

Abhishek smiled and began. "First of all, you need to accept that life is never static. It is full of highs and lows. There will be moments of success and moments of failure. But here's the thing—whenever we fall, life always gives us a chance to rise again. It may be through an indication, a reflection, a conversation with someone wiser, or even through introspection. But most people don't take that opportunity. They don't recognize the signs or believe that anything can be done about their situation. And so, they take their problems from bad to worse."

Mrs. Amby listened intently, nodding in agreement. "That's interesting," she said. "But what do you think keeps people trapped in this cycle? Why don't they break free?"

"Ah," Abhishek continued, "a lot of it depends on preconceived notions—our beliefs, perceptions, and attitudes. We make decisions based on how we perceive ourselves and the world around us. These perceptions become the shackles that limit us. We believe we can't change, so we don't try."

Mrs. Amby was silent for a moment, processing his words. Then, looking out at the horizon, she asked, "So, Abhishek, what would you say is the biggest tragedy in the world?"

Abhishek paused, taking in the question, before replying with a thoughtful smile, "The greatest tragedy, Amby, is that we grow old too soon and wise too late."

Mrs. Amby was surprised by the answer. "That's a bold statement. How do you mean?"

Abhishek turned to her, his eyes reflecting the wisdom of someone who had seen the truth in his own life. "Think about it. We spend our youth chasing fleeting pleasures, unaware of how quickly time passes. We waste time without purpose or care. And before we know it, we're older, but not wiser. By the time we realize how valuable time truly is, we're already too far along in life to change the course of things. That's the tragedy—time slips away, and we only regret how we spent it when it's too late."

He glanced around at the people on the beach. "Take a moment to observe those around us. Many are enjoying themselves, relaxing, and finding ways to destress. This break from their daily routines is essential—it's their way of breaking free from mental shackles and lightening the burdens they've carried for so long. Such moments of rejuvenation are necessary to regain clarity and energy. However, true fulfilment lies in channeling this renewed energy into purposeful actions that bring value to our lives and others. Successful individuals often stand apart because they manage their time and energy effectively, focusing on meaningful pursuits. The key to thriving is not just in taking breaks but in using those moments as a foundation for greater growth, meaningful pursuits and impact."

Mrs. Amby was deep in thought. "So, success... it's not about luck? It's about how we perceive ourselves and how we spend our time?"

"Exactly," Abhishek replied. "Success is not random. It is a result of our habits, our beliefs, and the decisions we make every day. But here's the kicker: our habits are often the shackles that hold us back. We live in a comfort zone, controlled by routine. Our habits become automatic, and before we know it, we stop questioning them. We stop thinking big. And those habits—they're like mental chains, preventing us from realizing our true potential."

Mrs. Amby nodded slowly, her mind whirring with the implications of what Abhishek was saying. "So, you're saying that the way we think—our beliefs and habits—creates these shackles that bind us?"

"Yes," Abhishek affirmed. "The mind is the first prison we build. Our limiting beliefs, our self-doubt, our fear of failure—they are the bars that keep us locked in. We believe we can't change, and so we don't. But the truth is, we can break free. We just have to see the shackles for what they are."

"Then how do we break free?" Mrs. Amby asked, eager to know more.

Abhishek smiled. "The first step is awareness. Once you understand that you are the one who has built these shackles, only then can you start dismantling them. Start with your thoughts, challenge your beliefs, and change your habits. It's not easy, but it's the only way to break free and live life on your own terms."

The waves continued to crash on the shore as the couple stood there, lost in thought. For the first time, Mrs. Amby felt a deep understanding of the silent forces that shaped her life. She realized that the shackles she had been wearing for so long were not made of metal, but of her own beliefs, fears, and limitations. And now, with this new understanding, the possibility of freedom seemed within reach. The first step toward breaking free had already begun.

As they continued their walk along the beach, the cool breeze felt like a symbol of fresh possibilities. The journey ahead was clear—if they could only find the strength to break the shackles of their own minds, the world was theirs to shape.

Lesson TWO

Unbroken Shackles: The Root Cause of Our Mental Chains

As time passes, there is a natural tendency to become more self-centred, more focused on our individual desires and comparisons with others. Take children, for example. They constantly want the latest gadgets—whether it's the newest mobile phone, the latest bicycle, or the trendiest clothes. If they don't get what they want, frustration sets in. They begin to think negatively, feeling that they are less privileged than their peers. This sense of entitlement, combined with unmet desires, slowly forms the first mental blocks—the early shackles of the mind.

These mental blocks, though seemingly harmless at first, begin to consume their energy. Instead of focusing on what truly matters, their thoughts get lost in a cycle of comparison and dissatisfaction. They become attached to false notions of success, believing that material possessions or status symbols are the only markers of happiness. Over time, they begin to accept their circumstances as they are, surrendering to the belief that they are not capable of achieving more. This lack of self-belief becomes another shackle, and with each passing year, it tightens its grip on their mind.

Shackles are formed when life lacks a clear purpose. A person without direction is like a ship without a rudder, drifting aimlessly through life. The root cause of these shackles lies in negative thinking, a mindset that distracts us from our true mission or task. This kind of thinking prevents us from focusing on what is essential and important. In today's world, distractions abound—from phone calls and messages to social media and endless distractions. We allow these interruptions to take us off course, leaving us with little to show for our time and energy.

Abhishek turned to Mrs. Amby with a serious expression. "The issue is simple, Amby. If we don't separate ourselves from distractions, those distractions will eventually separate us from our goals—and from the life we truly want."

Mrs. Amby nodded in agreement; her brow furrowed in thought. "Yes, I can see that. But how do we stop ourselves from falling into that trap?"

Abhishek smiled, recognizing the dawning understanding in her eyes. "The first thing is to protect your focus. For example, when you're working on something important, keep your phone out of reach. Put it in another room if necessary. You need to create an environment where distractions are minimized. It's not easy, I know, but it's necessary. We cannot allow distractions to take over our lives."

He paused, letting the weight of his words sink in. "But this is just the surface. The deeper issue lies in our negative thinking, the thoughts that feed our fears and insecurities. Every negative thought you entertain generates a shackle, a mental block that keeps you from moving forward."

Mrs. Amby listened intently, her mind already piecing together the connection between negative thoughts and the mental chains that bound her.

Abhishek continued, "And these shackles are not just the product of our adult lives. Many of them come from our childhood, from the way we were brought up. We carry forward these limiting beliefs, these false ideas about ourselves, and they shape the way we see the world. Let me tell you a story to illustrate how these mental blocks are formed and why we continue to hold on to them."

Mrs. Amby looked at him expectantly as he began the tale.

"There was once a king who, every morning before dawn, would ride through his kingdom to ensure that everything was in order. One morning, he came across an old man walking along the road carrying a heavy stone on his back. The king, curious, asked the man why he was carrying the stone at such an early hour when everyone else was asleep. But the old man, startled by the king's voice, panicked and fled, leaving the stone behind in the middle of the road."

Abhishek paused, making sure Mrs. Amby was following. She nodded, and he continued.

"The king waited for a while, hoping the man would return to collect the stone, but he never came back. The king eventually gave up and rode away, forgetting about the incident. But the stone stayed where it had fallen, right in the middle of the road. Over time, the stone became a significant obstacle, causing problems for travellers who passed through. It was no longer just a stone; it became a hindrance, an unwelcome obstruction.

"As time went on, people began to realize that the stone served no purpose other than to create trouble for those passing byers. They decided it should be removed. So, a group of people went to the new king, the son of the original monarch, to request that the stone be removed."

Abhishek paused again, letting the story sink in.

"But here's where it gets interesting," he said. "The new king, now on the throne, refused. He said, 'My father, the old king, had ordered that stone to be placed there. Only he could have ordered its removal.' So, the stone remained—unwanted, unnecessary, but stubbornly fixed in place. And no one could remove it."

Mrs. Amby raised an eyebrow. "But why? It was clearly causing harm. Why didn't they just get rid of it?"

Abhishek sighed. "Exactly. That stone became a symbol of something much larger—a mental block, a shackle, that served no real purpose but continued to exist because of old beliefs, unchallenged traditions, and the reluctance to change. It became an iconic landmark, not because it was useful, but because it had always been there. And that's what happens in our lives too, Amby. We create shackles—mental blocks—that serve no real purpose but continue to bind us because we've accepted them as part of our reality. We grow accustomed to them, and before we know it, they are in the way of our progress, and we don't even think to remove them."

Mrs. Amby took a deep breath. "So, these mental blocks we carry are like the stone in the road—they hold us back, even though they don't serve us in any way. But we keep them there because we've always had them, or because they've become familiar."

"Exactly," Abhishek replied. "We get so used to our beliefs, our habits, and our fears that we stop questioning them. We stop asking ourselves whether they are helping us or hindering us. And that's how we keep building these shackles—unwittingly, day by day."

"So, how do we remove them?" Mrs. Amby asked, her voice filled with determination.

Abhishek smiled. "The first step is to recognize them. To identify the beliefs, the habits, and the fears that are holding you back. Then, you can begin the work of dismantling them, one by one. It's not easy, but it is necessary. The road to freedom begins with awareness. Once you see the stone in your path, you can finally remove it."

The waves crashed softly against the shore as the conversation lingered in the air. For the first time, Mrs. Amby felt a sense of clarity—a new understanding of the invisible forces that had been shaping her life. And as she walked beside Abhishek, she realized that the journey to freedom was not about waiting for the world to change. It was about changing the way she saw the world—and breaking the shackles that had been holding her back for far too long.

Lesson THREE

How Are the Shackles Formed?

The next day, Mrs. Amby and Abhishek returned to the same spot on the beach where they had continued their conversation the day before. The discussion was taking shape in such a way that it felt like the beginning of something transformative. The cool breeze kissed their skin, and the sound of the waves lapping against the shore added a soothing backdrop to their exchange.

Mrs. Amby, still absorbed in their previous conversation, was eager to explore deeper truths about life and how they could break free from their own mental shackles. With a curious gleam in her eyes, she turned to Abhishek to continue their dialogue.

"Abhishek," she began, her voice filled with both enthusiasm and curiosity, "I've been thinking a lot about what we discussed yesterday. It makes so much sense. But tell me, besides negative or wrong thinking, are there other factors that contribute to the formation of these shackles we carry around in our minds?"

Abhishek smiled, appreciating her interest and eagerness to delve deeper. He took a moment to reflect, then responded thoughtfully.

"You know, Mrs. Amby," he began, "let me put it this way: the root cause of almost every problem we face—whether it's in our personal lives, careers, or health—is negative thinking. With each negative thought, a subtle shackle is woven into our mind. It forms a unique mindset, one that limits our growth and shapes our reality. Our mindset is what ultimately shapes our destiny. We are all, in a sense, limited by the beliefs we carry, especially the ones that come from negativity and fear."

He paused, looking at the horizon as if gathering his thoughts. "But aside from negative thinking, there are several other factors that continuously weave these shackles, sometimes without us even realizing it."

Mrs. Amby nodded, eager to hear more.

Abhishek continued, his tone steady and informative. "Take, for example, **Lack of Sleep**. Chronic sleep deprivation has become a serious issue in today's world, especially with so many of us constantly working late, staring at screens, or overloading our minds with stress. Sleep is crucial for cognitive function, memory, and concentration. When we don't get enough rest, our brain doesn't have the chance to rejuvenate and refresh itself. Over time, this can lead to long-term cognitive decline and mental health issues, weakening our ability to think clearly and make rational decisions. It's like slowly building a mental shackle that tightens with every sleepless night."

Mrs. Amby absorbed this information carefully. "I didn't realize that lack of sleep could have such a deep effect on our brain. What else contributes to these shackles?"

Abhishek nodded and went on. "Another factor is **Poor Diet**. Look at the way many young people today are eating. A diet high in processed foods, sugars, and unhealthy fats can seriously harm both our body and mind. It causes inflammation in the brain, which is linked to conditions like dementia and Alzheimer's disease. Over time, poor nutrition weakens your mental clarity and focus, which can prevent you from achieving your goals. This, too, becomes a shackle, hindering your ability to perform at your best."

Mrs. Amby frowned, her mind beginning to make the connections. "So, what we eat directly impacts our mental health as well?"

"Exactly," Abhishek said. "A poor diet doesn't just affect our physical health—it has a profound impact on our mental and emotional well-being. Our brain needs proper nutrition to function optimally. When it doesn't get what it needs, it becomes sluggish, and our ability to think, learn, and focus suffers."

He paused for a moment before adding another point. "Next is the **Sedentary Lifestyle** and **Excessive Screen Time**. We live in an era where most people spend hours sitting at a desk or glued to their phones or TVs. This lack of movement not only harms our physical health but also affects our mental agility. Sitting for long hours without regular exercise reduces blood flow to the brain and negatively impacts cognitive development. If you don't move your body, your mind becomes less agile over time. And excessive screen time, especially when done mindlessly, leads to a lack of engagement with real life. It's a vicious cycle—people get more sedentary, and their mental and emotional health deteriorates as a result."

Mrs. Amby was shocked. "I never realized that just sitting around could affect our brain so much. Is there any way to reverse this? Can we improve our mental fitness while living such a busy life?"

Abhishek smiled, seeing her concern. "Yes, of course! The solution lies in developing good habits and cultivating discipline. It's not about doing everything perfectly, but about taking consistent steps every day to uplift ourselves physically, mentally, and emotionally."

He leaned forward slightly, speaking with quiet confidence. "For example, engaging in activities that challenge your brain—such as puzzles, reading, or learning a new skill—helps keep your mind sharp. Mental stimulation is just as important as physical exercise. By constantly engaging our minds, we improve cognitive function and keep mental decline at bay."

Mrs. Amby nodded, absorbing his words. "So, keeping our brains active is just as important as keeping our bodies active. What about emotional health? How does that tie into these shackles?"

Abhishek's expression softened. "Ah, that's a critical point. **Neglecting mental health** issues like depression, anxiety, or prolonged stress can have long-lasting effects. Prolonged exposure to stress causes the brain to release hormones like cortisol, which over time can damage the brain's structure and its ability to function properly. This is why mental health needs to be taken seriously. If you're constantly under stress, your cognitive abilities, decision-making, and emotional resilience are severely impacted. Ignoring this emotional aspect only strengthens the shackles in your mind."

Mrs. Amby, now deep in thought, looked at Abhishek with a new sense of clarity. "So, it's not just negative thinking that forms these shackles. It's the combination of poor habits, lack of self-care, and not addressing mental and emotional health."

"Yes, indeed" Abhishek affirmed. "We often think of shackles as just thoughts, but they are also the result of how we treat our bodies and minds. It's the cumulative effect of all the distractions, bad habits, and neglect that slowly builds the chains that hold us back."

"That makes so much sense," Mrs. Amby said, feeling the weight of the conversation. "So, if we can break free from these habits—if we can take better care of our physical and mental health—then we can break the shackles and unlock our true potential?"

"Absolutely," Abhishek replied. "The good news is, it's never too late to start making changes. By consciously taking steps to improve our lifestyle, our habits, and our mindset, we can begin to break free from the shackles that limit us. It's all about small, consistent efforts that compound over time."

Mrs. Amby smiled, feeling a renewed sense of purpose. "I see now. It's not just about breaking free from negative thinking. It's about breaking free from the things that drain us—physically, mentally, and emotionally."

"Exactly," Abhishek said with a nod. "And once you start breaking free from these shackles, you'll begin to feel lighter, more focused, and more in control of your life. It's a process, but every step you take will lead you closer to the freedom and growth you deserve."

As the conversation came to an end, Mrs. Amby stood up and looked out over the vast expanse of the ocean. She felt a sense of clarity and motivation that she hadn't felt in a long time. The shackles, once invisible, were now clearly in view—and the path to breaking them was clearer than ever.

The waves crashed gently against the shore, a metaphor for the steady, gradual progress that lay ahead. For the first time, Mrs. Amby realized that breaking the shackles wasn't just about overcoming a few mental blocks—it was about taking control of her life, mind, and body, and making choices that aligned with her true potential.

Lesson FOUR

How to Prevent and Consistently Reduce the Effect of Shackles

Mrs. Amby sat quietly, a deep sense of relief washing over her. It was as if a veil had been lifted from her mind, revealing a clearer path forward. She felt a renewed sense of purpose, an almost spiritual shift—like she had discovered a key to a more fulfilling life. Yet, despite the clarity she had gained, there was still one question lingering in her mind. She turned to Abhishek, her voice thoughtful.

"Abhishek," she began, "I feel like I'm on the right track now, but there's still something I'm struggling to understand. How can we **prevent** the formation of these shackles in the first place? And, as I understand it, in our day-to-day life too, we'll always have to keep on **reducing the effects** of the shackles as they arise, won't we?"

Abhishek smiled, clearly amused by her thoughtful question. "You're absolutely right, Mrs. Amby. It's one thing to recognize the shackles and break free from them is another, but the real challenge is prevention and consistency. You can only prevent or reduce the effects of shackles by making yourself stronger—physically, mentally, emotionally, and even spiritually. More than 50% of your problems can be solved by developing **self-awareness, self-control** and discipline. But that requires building good habits and shedding bad ones."

He leaned back slightly, as if collecting his thoughts, before continuing. "Let me tell you this: there are numerous small habits, daily practices, that when repeated consistently, can have a massive return on your life. These habits, if ingrained into your routine, will help you stay on track and prevent the formation of shackles that limit your growth. So, let me give you a list of some habits that can change your life if practiced regularly."

Mrs. Amby listened intently, eager to absorb every word. Abhishek began his list:

1. **Set Your Goals Thoughtfully:** Establish clear, specific goals and do whatever it takes to achieve them. This creates a sense of purpose.

2. **Break Down Goals into Manageable Steps:** Break large goals into smaller tasks so you can see where you need to focus your energy.
3. **Track Your Time:** For one entire day, track every activity down to the minute. Identify where you're wasting time and eliminate those distractions.
4. **Audit Yourself Daily:** Before bed, review how much time and effort you've spent working towards your goals. This reflection keeps you accountable.
5. **Read Every Day:** Even if it's just one page, reading will continuously improve your knowledge and mental sharpness.
6. **Write Something Every Day:** Even if it's just one paragraph, writing daily keeps your mind active and creative.
7. **Write Down Your Ideas:** Write down anything that resonates with you. Our brains are for having ideas, not holding them.
8. **Value Your Time:** Protect your time as if it were the most precious resource, because it truly is.
9. **Keep Your Phone Away While Working:** If you're working or studying, keep your phone out of the room. Focus is essential for progress.
10. **Limit Your To-Do List:** Narrow down your daily tasks to the top 3 most important ones. Focus on what really matters.
11. **Listen More Than You Speak:** This creates space for learning and growth. Active listening also helps in building meaningful relationships.
12. **Create More Than You Consume:** Don't just passively consume information; engage with it, apply it, and create something of your own.
13. **Get Sunlight Early:** Spend time outdoors, ideally in the morning, to regulate your body's rhythm and boost your mood.

14. **Take Breaks When You're Mentally Drained:** When your brain feels fatigued, take a break. Disconnect for a few minutes and come back refreshed.
15. **Engage in Hobbies:** Find hobbies that stimulate both your mind and soul, and do them regularly. This promotes a healthy balance between work and play.
16. **Compliment More Than You Complain:** Shift your focus towards positivity. Compliment others genuinely, and it will reflect back on you.
17. **Simplify Your Life:** Delete apps and donate clothes that you no longer use. This helps clear mental and physical clutter.
18. **Serve Others:** Helping others is a powerful way to bring joy and fulfilment into your life.
19. **Reconnect with Old Friends:** Make a habit of reaching out to old friends. Meaningful connections nurture emotional well-being.
20. **Learn to Say No:** Don't say yes just because you feel obligated. Set boundaries that protect your time and energy.
21. **Control Your Information Diet:** Be mindful of what you consume mentally. Junk information can be as harmful to your mind as junk food is to your body.
22. **Revisit Joyful Experiences:** Look back at things that have brought you happiness in the past. Reconnect with what makes you feel good.
23. **Set Time Limits on Tasks:** Use Parkinson's Law—work expands to fill the time available for its completion. Set deadlines and stick to them.

Mrs. Amby's eyes widened in surprise. "Oh my God, that list is endless!" she exclaimed. "But it's also fantastic! Everything you mentioned is within our power to do. We can simply incorporate these habits into our daily routines, one by one." Also, tell me more about Parkinson's Law, you have just mentioned. I am quite curious to know about it.

Abhishek chuckled, pleased with her enthusiasm. "Exactly. But first be on habits; these habits may seem small, but over time, they have a massive impact. It's about making conscious choices every day to move towards a better, more fulfilling life. The more you practice these habits, the stronger you'll become—mentally, physically, and emotionally." Now let's talk about Parkinson's Law on time management. The Concept of Parkinson's Law was first described by a British Historian and Author Mr Cyril Northcote Parkinson in 1955. He later wrote a book about the concept, titled "Parkinson's Law: the pursuit of Progress". According to this Law, People have tendency to adjust their pace according to the amount of time they have to finish it. For Example- If you have a two-week deadline to complete a project, you might take longer than necessary to finish it.

Mrs. Amby nodded thoughtfully and said understood. "But, Abhishek, do you think we need to follow a specific routine to start the day? Like, some kind of morning ritual?"

Abhishek smiled; glad she was picking up on the details. "Yes, Mrs. Amby, that's a great question. A strong morning routine sets the tone for the rest of the day. When you start your day right, you're more likely to be productive, focused, and in control. Here's what I would recommend as a powerful morning ritual."

He spoke with conviction, outlining the steps:

1. **Wake Up Early (5-6 AM):** This gives you a head start on the day. Early risers tend to be more productive and mentally sharp. See, each time you rise at dawn, you will

purify your character, fortify your will-power and magnify the fire of the soul.

2. **Hydrate yourself:** Drink a glass of water as soon as you wake up to rehydrate your body and kickstart your metabolism.
3. **Exercise:** Hit the gym or engage in 20 minutes of yoga, stretching, or running. Physical activity is crucial for both body and brain health.
4. **Read a book or Learn Something New:** Dedicate at least 15 minutes to learning a new skill or gaining knowledge. This fosters mental growth.
5. **Write in a Journal:** Write down your thoughts, reflect on your goals, and clear any negativity that may be clouding your mind.
6. **Spend Time in Nature:** Go for a walk or simply step outside to get some fresh air and clear your mind. Nature has a calming effect on the soul.
7. **Plan Your Day:** Review your goals for the day and prioritize your tasks. Setting clear intentions in the morning brings clarity to the rest of your day.

Mrs. Amby absorbed these suggestions carefully. "This morning ritual sounds like exactly what I need," she said, smiling. "I can see how these habits would create a strong foundation for the rest of the day."

Abhishek nodded. "I'm glad you find it helpful. Morning rituals are crucial, but so is regular maintenance. It's important to detox your mind and soul, especially if you've recognized that you're dealing with deep-rooted shackles. Once you start to break free, it's essential to cleanse yourself regularly to stay on track."

Mrs. Amby was curious. "Is there a specific way to detox the mind and soul, Abhishek?"

Abhishek's smile deepened. "Absolutely, Mrs. Amby. Let's dive into that in our next conversation."

As the waves rolled gently onto the shore, Mrs. Amby felt a sense of anticipation for the next chapter in their discussion. She had learned so much already, but there was more to uncover—more tools, more strategies, more wisdom to help her break free from the shackles that had held her back for so long. And with that thought, she felt the first stirrings of true freedom.

Lesson FIVE

How to Eliminate & Detox the Mind of Shackles

The sun was setting on another beautiful day in Goa, casting long golden rays across the beach. Mrs. Amby and Abhishek had met once again to continue their conversation about life, habits, and self-improvement. As they sat on the sand, the sound of the waves in the background, Abhishek began with an important cautionary note.

"You know, Mrs. Amby," he began, looking thoughtfully out at the horizon, "ordinary people can accomplish extraordinary things once they routinize the right habits. To truly find your best self, you have to let go of your worst self. One of the most powerful ways to do this is by **decluttering your mind-**

-detoxing it from the shackles that limit you. This mental detoxification is key to unlocking your full potential and attaining the freedom to live your life to the fullest."

Mrs. Amby leaned forward; her interest piqued. "I'm all ears, Abhishek. Tell me how I can detox my mind and eliminate these shackles that have been holding me back."

Abhishek smiled, glad to see her so engaged. "Alright, let me take you through **six essential ways** to cleanse your mind of shackles and set yourself free. Trust me, these practices are simple but powerful, and once you start, you'll feel the change almost immediately."

Mrs. Amby nodded, eager to hear more. "Please, go ahead. I'm ready."

1. Start Unfollowing:

"First and foremost," Abhishek began, "you must **unfollow** the negativity in your life. This includes both the people and the content you consume. Stop hanging around with people who aren't ambitious or who drain your energy. Unfollow those who don't inspire you or make you feel empowered. Whether it's on social media or in real life, remember that **blocking, muting, deleting**, or unfollowing is an act of **self-care**. It's essential to protect your energy and ensure you surround yourself with those who encourage your growth, not hinder it."

Mrs. Amby nodded thoughtfully, recognizing how social media often added unnecessary stress and comparisons to her life. "I see what you mean. It's about creating an environment that nourishes my mind."

"Exactly," Abhishek agreed. "You need to curate your surroundings consciously."

2. Be Selectively Social:
"Next, be **selectively social**. This means you should intentionally keep your social circle small, but meaningful. Focus on quality over quantity. The people you spend time with should be aligned with your values, aspirations, and goals. Your inner circle should be made up of people who encourage your personal growth, challenge you in positive ways, and support your ambitions."

Mrs. Amby smiled, her mind already thinking about some of her friendships that didn't serve her growth. "I get it. I've often been too concerned with keeping a large circle of friends, but perhaps it's time to focus on those who really add value to my life."

Abhishek nodded. "Yes, the fewer distractions, the more focused you can be on your own path."

3. Live in the Moment:
"One of the biggest sources of mental clutter is dwelling on the past or worrying about the future," Abhishek continued. "You can't change what's already happened, but you **can** shape your present. Stay grounded in the **here and now**. Shift your focus to the things that are within your control—your thoughts, your actions, your decisions. The past is gone, and the future is yet to come. All you have is the present moment. Make it count."

Mrs. Amby felt a deep sense of relief wash over her at this simple yet profound advice. "That's such a comforting thought, Abhishek. It's like the weight of the past and the fear of the future just dissipate when you focus on the present."

"Exactly," Abhishek said with a smile. "The present is where your power lies."

4. Eat Healthy:

"Next, let's talk about your physical health," Abhishek said. "The way you eat affects your mental state. **Eat healthy**, because when you eat nourishing foods, you're fuelling your brain for optimal function. And let's be honest—food is often an emotional crutch for many of us. But instead of turning to comfort food when stressed, shift towards a diet that supports both your physical and mental well-being. Healthy foods like vegetables, fruits, lean proteins, and whole grains nourish your body and mind."

Mrs. Amby was quick to agree. "I've noticed that when I eat junk food or indulge in emotional eating, I feel sluggish and mentally foggy. But when I eat clean and healthy, I feel lighter, more energized, and focused."

"Exactly," Abhishek said. "Your brain needs the right fuel to think clearly and stay sharp."

5. Meditate Alone:

Abhishek's tone softened as he spoke about one of the most important practices for mental clarity. "Next, it's crucial to spend time in **solitude. Meditate alone**, especially in the evening. A dark room with only the natural sounds of the world—whether it's the wind blowing, rain falling, or thunder rumbling—creates the perfect environment for clearing your mind. Meditation helps you connect with your deeper self, release tension, and reset your thoughts."

Mrs. Amby felt a sense of calm just hearing him describe the practice. "I've tried meditation before, but I never made it a habit. It's definitely something I can work on.

Just sitting quietly and letting go of everything seems so powerful."

Abhishek smiled. "It truly is. The mind can only rest and heal when it's given space to quiet down."

6. Take a Trip:
"Another way to detox your mind is to **take a trip**. Now, I'm not talking about a luxury vacation—just a simple getaway where you disconnect from the hustle and bustle of daily life. Go into nature, soak in the beauty of the surroundings, and let go of your everyday worries. A change of scenery, even for a day or two, can refresh your mind and provide new perspectives."

Mrs. Amby thought about how disconnected she felt from nature in her day-to-day life. "I love the idea of taking a short trip to get away from the noise of the city. Nature has always had a calming effect on me."

"It's a simple but profound way to detox," Abhishek said. "Sometimes, stepping away is the best way to find clarity."

7. Avoid Habits That Make You Weak:
Abhishek continued, now getting to some of the more challenging aspects of mental detox. "Next, you need to **avoid habits** that make you weak. These can include trying to control everything, falling into a negative mindset, or neglecting to express yourself confidently. Practice **assertiveness** when needed, and make sure you are maintaining **cordial relationships** with those around you. However, while focusing on personal relationships, don't lose sight of your career goals and aspirations. Balance is key."

Mrs. Amby nodded. "Sometimes, I try to control situations too much, and that causes stress. Letting go of that control seems like a good way to ease my mind."

Abhishek smiled. "You're on the right track. Let go of what you can't control and focus on what you can."

8. Avoid Procrastination and Excuses:
Abhishek's voice took on a firmer tone. "Procrastination and excuses are toxic for your brain. These are signs of a lack of discipline and confidence. 'I'll start tomorrow,' 'I'm too tired,' 'I don't have time,' 'It's too hard'—these are all **mental shackles**. You need to confront them head-on. The longer you put things off, the harder it becomes to break free."

Mrs. Amby's face lit up as she realized the truth in his words. "I've been guilty of putting things off, but I see now how it just compounds the stress and keeps me stuck."

Abhishek nodded. "Exactly. The sooner you take action, the sooner you free yourself."

9. Start Writing:
Finally, Abhishek offered a powerful tool for dealing with overthinking. "When your mind is racing, start **writing**. If you're overthinking or feeling overwhelmed, write it all down. Do a brain dump. Clear out the nagging thoughts and worries. Set a timer for 30 minutes, and let your thoughts flow onto paper. It's a simple but effective way to detox your mind."

Mrs. Amby laughed. "I've always loved journaling, but I never realized how therapeutic it could be for clearing out mental clutter."

Abhishek grinned. "Writing is one of the most powerful ways to process and release your thoughts."

Mrs. Amby sat back, absorbing the wisdom she had just received. "Abhishek, this is exactly what I needed to hear. Detoxing the mind, eliminating these shackles—this is how we start living our best lives, isn't it?"

Abhishek smiled warmly, "Yes, it is. And remember, detoxing your mind is not a one-time fix. It's a daily practice. Just like physical health, mental health requires consistent care and attention."

Mrs. Amby smiled, feeling a deep sense of clarity and purpose. "I'm ready to start. Thank you for opening my eyes to all this. I'm excited to begin the journey of true freedom."

Abhishek nodded. "You're welcome, Mrs. Amby. The journey has already begun."

And with that, they both stood up and walked along the beach.

Lesson SIX

How to Come Out of Shackles

The sun was beginning to dip below the horizon, casting a warm, golden hue across the peaceful Goan beach. A gentle breeze swept through the air, brushing against the faces of Mr. Abhishek and Mrs. Amby as they stood hand in hand, savouring the serenity of the moment. The wind tousled Amby's hair, which fluttered around her face, giving her an almost ethereal, otherworldly beauty. She looked up at Abhishek, her eyes bright with excitement, and said, "How I wish, Abhishek, that I could have lived this blissful life in my past too. But that would have been possible only if I had known about these Shackles, the mental blocks you mentioned earlier."

Abhishek listened intently; his expression thoughtful. After a brief pause, he squeezed her hand gently. "Don't worry, Amby," he replied with conviction. "I'll show you the way to break free from these shackles, and once you understand how, you'll never be trapped by them again."

He turned to face her more fully, his voice steady. "The key, as I told you before, is awareness. Awareness is the first step to breaking free. You need to do things on the principle of 'first time right.' But it's not just about awareness—it's about developing a strong character. You need discipline, commitment, and confidence. These qualities are your foundation."

Amby listened closely; her curiosity piqued.

"For example," Abhishek continued, "one of the most powerful tools you can develop is knowing when to speak and when to remain silent. Learning this can cut out many unnecessary problems in life." He paused for a moment to let his words sink in.

"Sometimes, silence is more powerful than words. You should remain silent if you don't have the full story. If you're too emotional to think clearly, silence is often the wisest choice. When you're in the heat of anger or when your words could hurt someone or damage a friendship, silence can save the relationship. And, in some cases, silence can preserve entire bonds."

He smiled as he quoted an old proverb: "Speech is silver, silence is golden."

Amby nodded; her expression thoughtful. "I understand, Abhishek. But what about confidence? How do I build that?"

Abhishek's eyes softened with understanding, and he took a deep breath before answering. "Ah, confidence. Without confidence, success is impossible. It's the belief that you can succeed that fuels every action. To build confidence, there are a few key steps you need to follow."

"First," he said, "you need to learn a high-value skill—something that will set you apart and increase your value in the world. This will directly increase your cash flow and, more importantly, your self-esteem."

He paused, making sure she was following. "Second, surround yourself with people who are on the right path—people who uplift you, not those who bring you down. Avoid distractions that waste your time and energy."

"Work on yourself every single day," he added. "The key is consistent, incremental improvement. And as you grow, make sure you become independent. Don't rely on others to validate you or dictate your path.

"Replace bad habits with good ones. If you want to change your life, you have to change your habits. Remove negative thoughts from your mind. They are the shackles that hold you back. Instead, use your mistakes—and even your anger—as fuel to drive you forward, to get better and better at everything you do."

He leaned in a little closer, his voice firm and confident. "Create an abundance mindset. Believe that there is always more—more opportunity, more success, more growth. The world is full of possibilities, but you have to be open to them."

Amby took a deep breath, feeling a surge of clarity and resolve. She had always known there was more to life, more to her potential, but hearing Abhishek lay out the path so clearly made her believe it was possible. Slowly, she smiled, feeling a sense of possibility that she had never felt before.

"I see now," she said softly, "how breaking free from these shackles is the first step to a life of freedom. Thank you, Abhishek. For showing me the way."

Abhishek smiled back; his heart full of pride for her. "It's just the beginning, Amby. The journey ahead is yours to take. But remember, the freedom you seek is within you, and it's only a matter of learning how to break the chains you've been holding onto for so long."

And as they stood there on that quiet beach, hand in hand, the horizon stretched before them, full of limitless possibilities.

Lesson SEVEN

How to Maintain a Shackle-Free Blissful Life

The sun was setting on another day at the beach, casting a soft glow over the water. The gentle waves lapped at the shore, and the breeze carried the scent of salt and freedom. Mrs. Amby, who had been soaking in the peaceful atmosphere, couldn't shake her curiosity. The questions that had once seemed endless now had clear answers, but there was still one lingering in her mind—a crucial one that she had to ask.

Turning to Abhishek, she asked, "Abhishek, all that you've said makes so much sense. But tell me, how do you maintain a shackle-free life once you've recognized the shackles and broken free from them? What's the next step?"

Abhishek, seemingly amused by her insatiable curiosity, grinned and replied, "Ah, Amby, I thought you had no more questions. But here we are, and you've surprised me with another very important one! Okay, let me answer that for you."

He paused for a moment, choosing his words carefully before continuing. "To maintain a shackle-free life, you have to adopt a particular lifestyle. It's not just about breaking free from the chains; it's about constantly reinforcing the freedom you've gained. And that comes from building a strong personality and character. You can only do that by keeping your word, making time for what truly matters, and fearlessly saying 'no' to things that don't serve you."

Amby nodded, absorbing his words, and Abhishek went on, his tone firm yet encouraging.

"You've got to live with intention, Amby. That means living according to your values, not the expectations of others. For example, when it comes to your appearance—wear clothes that fit you well, that suit your body and style. I'm not saying you need to wear designer labels, but tailored clothes will help you feel confident and look sharp. When you take care of the way you present yourself, you automatically feel more empowered and in control. And remember, confidence is key."

Amby listened intently, eager to learn more.

"You should also be the kind of person who admits mistakes honestly," Abhishek continued. "It takes courage, but owning your errors and learning from them is essential for personal growth. Never shy away from responsibility, especially when things go wrong. Be the first to reach out when there's a problem, and take the initiative to resolve it."

He looked at her, his expression serious. "Confidence doesn't mean arrogance. It's about leading, not following for the sake of it. Don't argue just to argue. Stand firm in your beliefs, but always speak the truth, even when it's hard. And be decisive. When you know something is right, take the lead and move forward."

Amby smiled, impressed by his wisdom. "That makes sense. But what about other impactful things like food and physical well-being?"

Abhishek raised an eyebrow, then nodded. "Good question. If you know how to cook, that's a huge advantage. Relying on others to prepare your meals can lead to disappointment, especially if you're not satisfied with what's on your plate. By being self-sufficient in the kitchen, you eliminate one source of potential frustration and, ultimately, the formation of shackles."

"And," he added, "a strong body and a resilient mindset are equally important. You can't be shackled by fear if you've trained yourself to fight, to defend your peace, and to be physically strong. A healthy body supports a healthy mind."

Amby looked thoughtful. "So, it's about being prepared in every aspect of life?"

Abhishek smiled. "Exactly. Once you've laid that foundation of personal strength and self-sufficiency, the next step is to build a lifestyle of discipline. And it all starts with problem-solving. You have to set clear and achievable goals that give direction to your life. Without goals, you'll wander aimlessly, creating unnecessary chaos. But with purpose, you can address problems effectively."

He continued, "Develop critical thinking. Don't just react to situations—analyze them. Consider different perspectives before making decisions. You have to develop the habit of objectivity and always approach problems with a clear mind."

Amby's eyes lit up as she connected the dots. "I see. It's about building a mindset that tackles life's challenges strategically, rather than reacting impulsively."

Abhishek nodded in agreement. "Exactly. And there's more to it. Another key aspect of a shackle-free life is effective communication. You must be able to express yourself clearly, both verbally and in writing. That's how you resolve conflicts, build strong relationships, and ensure that your voice is heard when it matters. Learn to listen, too. Communication isn't just about speaking; it's about understanding others as well."

Amby absorbed his words, feeling a deeper understanding take root. "So, it's about developing the ability to handle every situation with wisdom, and not letting it tie us down."

"Precisely," Abhishek said, nodding. "But there's one more thing to remember. To maintain a shackle-free life, you must adopt a growth mindset. Commit to lifelong learning. The world is constantly changing, and to stay free from new shackles, you have to grow with it. Every challenge, every setback, is an opportunity to learn and improve."

"Adaptability," Amby said, her voice firm with realization. "The ability to adapt to change and bounce back from setbacks is crucial."

Abhishek smiled. "Yes, exactly. If you can stay flexible and find alternative solutions when obstacles arise, you'll never form new shackles. Life will always present challenges, but your ability to adapt will ensure you don't get stuck in any situation."

"And don't forget time management," he added. "Prioritize tasks and manage your time wisely. Procrastination is the enemy of freedom. It piles on unnecessary stress and creates more problems. Stay organized, and tackle each task with intention. A shackle-free life is not just about mental freedom—it's about mastering your time and your responsibilities."

Amby exhaled slowly, feeling the weight of his words settling in. "So, to maintain a shackle-free life, it's not just about breaking the chains—it's about continuous self-improvement, discipline, and the ability to navigate life's challenges with grace and wisdom."

Abhishek smiled warmly. "Exactly. Life will always throw new challenges your way, Amby. But with the right mindset, preparation, and skills, you'll be able to maintain that shackle-free bliss forever."

They stood in silence for a moment, looking out at the horizon, knowing that the journey ahead was one of constant growth—a journey that would take them further into the freedom they had always dreamed of.

Lesson EIGHT

Finally... Affirmations & The Pledge

And finally... Amby, her eyes glimmering with a mix of curiosity and determination, stated, "Well, Abhishek, I've been listening to you intently. We've delved into various issues responsible for our silent downfall if we fail to become aware. It has been nothing short of enlightening. Your insights have awakened something profound within me, and for that, I'm deeply grateful. But now, I have one final question for you: '*How can we remain the best version of ourselves on a day-to-day basis?*'"

Abhishek smiled warmly, acknowledging the significance of her question. “Ah, Amby, that’s not just a question but a concluding thought to our dialogue. It’s the ultimate key to sustaining growth and excellence.”

He leaned forward slightly, his tone firm yet encouraging. “First and foremost, you must take care of your mind, body, and soul. Protect your energy, move in silence, set your boundaries, and stay committed to your goals. Every single day, focus entirely on the task at hand, applying your unique traits and skills to complete it effectively. This allows you to save both time and effort while preparing you for the next challenge as well.”

Amby nodded, visibly absorbing every word.

“And,” Abhishek continued, “it’s equally important to instil a daily habit of positive reinforcement. Start your day with affirmations and end it with reflection. Every night, ask yourself two vital questions before going to bed: **What is my goal?** and **how much time and effort did I invest today toward achieving that goal?** This keeps you aligned and accountable.”

“Interesting,” Amby said with a thoughtful smile. “But you mentioned something about a pledge earlier. Can you elaborate on that?”

Abhishek’s eyes lit up. “Ah, yes—the pledge. It’s more than just words on paper; it’s a powerful self-affirmation, a daily reminder of your commitment to becoming the best version of yourself. A degree may not define your intelligence, but discipline, focus, and a lifestyle rooted in strong principles will pave the way to unshakable success.”

He reached into his bag and handed her a sheet of paper, neatly formatted with bold words at the top: *MY PLEDGE.*

"This," he said, "is a framework. It's not set in stone—you can customize it to suit your personal journey. I suggest printing it, signing it, and keeping it somewhere visible—your desk, your mirror, or even your wallet. Trust me, Amby, its magical effects will manifest sooner than you think."

Mrs Amby is signing a pledge

My Pledge

I, *(your name)*, pledge my life to become unstoppable.

From today, I take full control of my mind, my thoughts, my body, and my life. I will never allow average thinking to hold me back.

- I will dream big and put in 10 times more effort to make my dreams a reality.
- I vow to eliminate negative influences, habits, and relationships from my life.
- I will only surround myself with ambitious, inspiring individuals.
- I will unlock the genius within me and share it with the world.
- I will win by helping others win and building lasting legacies.
- I will strive for excellence in my family life, health, and financial well-being.
- I will work hard, smart, and consistently, training my mind and body every single day.
- I will stop making excuses and take full responsibility for my life.
- I WILL MAKE BOTH MYSELF AND MY FAMILY PROUD OF ME.

I Pledge to become unstoppable.

Place: ____________________

Date: ____________________

Signature: ________________

Abhishek let the words sink in as Amby read the pledge aloud to herself, her voice resonating with determination.

"But remember," Abhishek added, "the pledge is only as effective as the effort you put into upholding it. Make it a daily ritual, and you'll notice transformative changes in no time."

Amby smiled, her face glowing with newfound resolve. "Thank you, Abhishek. This conversation has been nothing short of life-changing. I'm ready to embrace this pledge and make those affirmations a part of my daily life."

"Good," Abhishek replied, leaning back with satisfaction. "Because the journey to becoming unstoppable begins now."

Lesson NINE

The Aftermath of the Unbroken Shackles

"Amby, remember," Abhishek began, standing against the backdrop of the setting sun, "the pledge is deeply sacred. However, you can adapt it to align with your vision, what truly matters is your commitment to uphold it. Pair that with the nightly habit of asking yourself the two questions I shared earlier and that is *What is my goal?* And *how much effort have I invested today—or over the past week, fortnight, or month—to achieve it?* As you know now this practice is like a personal audit, keeping you honest, focused, and aligned with your progress."

Amby nodded thoughtfully, her eyes reflecting both gratitude and determination.

Abhishek continued, "The aftermath of breaking your shackles—the chains of blame, toxic influences, and ignorance—is liberation. You'll stop pointing fingers at others for your downfalls and start taking 100% responsibility for your life. With this mindset, you'll naturally distance yourself from toxic people who drain your energy and align yourself with those who uplift and inspire you."

Amby interjected with a newfound excitement. “That’s so true, Abhishek. "I’ve started noticing cracks in some friendships that no longer serve me well. It’s time to realign my focus and priorities."

Abhishek smiled and added, “You’ll also realize that financial independence is foundational. Lack of money often traps people in cycles of stress and despair, creating endless shackles. Ninety-nine percent of problems can be mitigated with financial discipline. Start investing early—money invested today buys back time tomorrow.”

Amby’s eyes lit up. “You know, Abhishek, I realized the power of money when I moved to Mumbai from Delhi in 2007. That decision forced me to rethink how I managed my finances. Since then, I’ve consistently invested in FDs and SIPs. It’s why I’m comfortable today—and your guidance along the way was invaluable.”

Abhishek acknowledged her progress with a nod. “You’ve been meticulous, Amby. It shows. But financial planning is just one piece. A fulfilling life requires a holistic approach—physical, mental, and emotional discipline. And this begins with a powerful daily routine.”

The Power of Rituals

Abhishek leaned forward; his voice filled with conviction. “Develop a habit of waking up early every morning. The world feels different at dawn—calmer, clearer, more energizing. Exercise daily, even if it’s just a brisk walk. Feed your mind by reading a few pages of a meaningful book every day. Write down your long-term goals regularly—it keeps you focused. Save money consistently, and surround yourself with capable, positive people.”

Amby listened intently, her resolve growing stronger. "Abhishek, your words are like a guiding light. They've swept away the dust of ignorance that clouded my mind and soul. I'm truly grateful."

Abhishek placed a hand on her shoulder, his expression warm. "It's my pleasure, Amby. You've been an irreplaceable support for me as well. But let me leave you with one more thought: Beyond routines and plans, what we all need most is care, love, and respect. Without these, life feels hollow."

Amby smiled and asked, "How do we maintain respect, though, especially when people have a tendency to take us for granted?"

The Essence of Respect

Abhishek's face lit up with approval. "That's an excellent question, Amby. Respect starts with self-respect. Never let others take it from you. Stop being overly available to people—it makes them undervalue your time. Stay away from negativity and always give respect if you expect it in return. Don't beg for favours, and most importantly, love yourself unconditionally."

He paused, then added, "Here are a few life lessons that will help maintain your dignity:

1. Don't share more than people need to know.
2. Avoid lending money to family or friends. If you give, don't expect it back.
3. Never insult the food or hospitality of others.
4. Refrain from taking out your phone during conversations—it's deeply disrespectful.
5. Don't take credit for work you didn't do.

6. Avoid making fun of friends in front of their children.
7. Never let emotions overpower your judgment.

And remember, Amby, always dress well, no matter the occasion. Your appearance reflects your respect for yourself and the moment. I know this is something you already excel at."

Amby laughed lightly. "You know me too well, Abhishek. I do take pride in dressing well."

A Moment of Reflection

As the waves lapped gently against the shore, they sat in silence, letting the cool sea breeze wash over them. Both seemed lost in thought, meditating on the truths they had uncovered together. The sea, vast and eternal, mirrored life itself—ever-changing yet constant in its lessons.

The Journey back Home

The next morning, as the sun rose over Goa, Amby and Abhishek prepared to return to Mumbai. Their hearts were lighter, their minds sharper, and their spirits filled with purpose. They left the serene shores with a renewed vision, a broadened outlook, and an unshakable determination to embrace the bright future that lay ahead. Together, they knew, they were ready to face whatever challenges awaited them—with clarity, resilience, and gratitude.

New day, new possibilities!!

Notes

Notes

www.ingramcontent.com/pod-product-compliance
Lightning Source LLC
LaVergne TN
LVHW090139160826
845673LV00017B/2514